A Mosaic of Nations

Indigenous North America Before 1500

John A. Cowgill

Illustrations by Caroline DeHaven

Published by
Cronos Creek Media
Berryville, Virginia

https://www.cronoscreek.com

ISBN: 978-1-945553-06-6
Printed in the USA

DEDICATION

To the vibrant tapestry of Indigenous peoples across North America, whose stories, resilience, and profound wisdom have shaped this land for millennia. May this book serve as a small step in honoring their enduring legacies, fostering understanding, and inspiring a new generation to listen, learn, and connect with the rich histories that have always been here. To the elders who carry the past, the youth who embrace the future, and the land that holds it all.

CONTENTS

For Teachers, Homeschoolers, and Students

For free materials related to Indigenous Cultures, visit us at:
https://cronoscreek.com/indigenous-America/study-guide

Your free study guide includes:

- **Teacher Guide**
- **Lesson Overview for 5 Key Topics**
- **Classroom Discussion Questions**
- **Map Activity**
- **Compare and Contrast Worksheet**
- **Timeline of Indigenous America**
- **Unit Test and Answer Key**

Preface

Imagine stepping back in time, not just a few years, but thousands of years, to a continent brimming with life, innovation, and incredible diversity. Before ships from distant lands arrived, this vast land we call North America was a home to countless nations, each with its own unique language, traditions, and ways of understanding the world. This book is an invitation to explore that incredible world, a world built by peoples who lived in harmony with the land, who developed ingenious solutions to life's challenges, and who created societies as complex and vibrant as any on Earth. We'll journey from the icy north to the sun-baked southwest, from the deep forests of the east to the vast grasslands of the plains. You'll meet people who built towering cities, others who navigated treacherous oceans in handmade canoes, and brilliant minds who forged lasting peace among nations. This is not a story of a single people, but a magnificent mosaic of hundreds of distinct cultures, each a vital thread in the rich fabric of North America's past. Our goal is to bring these stories to life for you, using language that's as clear and engaging as a conversation with a wise storyteller, making history feel not like a dusty old book, but like a thrilling adventure waiting to be discovered. We want you to see the ingenuity, the strength, and the deep connection to the natural world that defined these ancient societies, and to understand that their influence continues to resonate today.

Have you ever wondered what North America was like long before any of us were born, long before the cities and highways we know today? It was a place of breathtaking beauty and incredible variety, from towering mountains and ancient forests to sweeping plains and sun-drenched deserts. But more importantly, it was a place alive with people – hundreds of distinct Indigenous nations, each with their own languages, traditions, and ways of life. For thousands of years, these peoples called this land home. They weren't just living here; they were thriving. They developed amazing ways to build homes, hunt food, create art, and govern themselves, all while developing a deep and respectful connection with the natural world around them.

This book is your guide to discovering some of these incredible stories. We're going to travel across this vast continent and meet some of the ingenious people who shaped it. Think of it like exploring different neighborhoods, each with its own unique character and charm. We'll visit the Eastern Woodlands, where people lived in harmony with the forests and rivers, and marvel at the great cities built by the Mississippian culture along mighty waterways. We'll discover how people in the arid Southwest became masters of water and desert life, and how the bounty of the Pacific Northwest fueled vibrant cultures of art and community. We'll also venture to the Great Plains, where life revolved around the mighty bison, and journey north to the Arctic, where the Inuit people showed incredible resilience in a land of ice and snow. And we'll explore the remarkable political achievements of the Iroquois Confederacy, a powerful union of nations built on principles of peace and cooperation.

Our journey isn't just about learning facts; it's about understanding how these diverse peoples lived, what they valued, and how they adapted to their environments with incredible creativity. We'll try to make these stories come alive, using words that paint pictures and comparisons that help you connect with their experiences. We want you to see how similar their challenges and triumphs were to ours – the need for community, the drive to innovate, and the desire for a good life. This is a chance to expand your understanding of history and to appreciate the rich, complex, and enduring legacy of the First Peoples of North America. Let the adventure begin!

1 | A Vast and Ancient Land

Imagine a continent so vast it stretches from lands eternally kissed by ice to sun-baked realms where life clings fiercely to the earth. Picture towering mountains scraping the sky, mighty rivers carving pathways through ancient forests, and sprawling prairies whispering secrets on the wind. This was North America before the year 1500, a land of breathtaking beauty and incredible variety, a place that had been home to people for thousands upon thousands of years.

For millennia before the arrival of Europeans, this continent was not an empty wilderness waiting to be discovered, but a vibrant tapestry woven with countless human lives. These weren't just scattered groups; they were thriving nations, each with its own unique story, its own way of life, and its own deep understanding of the land they inhabited. It's easy to think of "Native Americans" as one single group, but that's like saying everyone in Europe is the same because they live on the same continent. The reality was far richer, far more diverse.

Consider the sheer scale of the land. In the far north, across what is now Canada and Alaska, lay the Arctic, a stark and stunning landscape of ice sheets, frozen seas, and a surprisingly resilient ecosystem. Here, life was a constant dance with the elements, a testament to human ingenuity in the face of extreme cold. Further south, vast forests dominated much of the eastern half of the continent, their dense canopies sheltering a rich array of plants and animals. These were the woodlands, a place of rivers and lakes, of abundant game and fertile soil, where communities flourished.

Moving westward, the land transformed dramatically. The Great Plains stretched out like an endless sea of grass, a seemingly boundless horizon where vast herds of bison roamed, shaping the lives of the people who lived alongside them. To the southwest, a dramatically different world unfolded. Here, the land was often arid, sculpted by wind and sun into dramatic canyons and mesas. Yet, life persisted, and in some of the driest regions, people developed ingenious ways to coax sustenance from the earth, building magnificent settlements in cliffs and valleys.

And then there were the coasts. The Pacific coast, with its temperate rainforests and rich marine life, offered a bounty that sustained sophisticated societies. The Atlantic coast, too, provided sustenance from the sea, as well as resources from the inland forests and waterways. Each of these regions, and countless others in between, presented unique challenges and opportunities, and the Indigenous peoples who called them home developed equally unique and remarkable ways of living.

This wasn't a static existence. These cultures weren't frozen in time. They were dynamic, evolving, and constantly adapting. Over thousands of years, people had migrated across the continent, driven by curiosity, by changing climates, by the pursuit of resources, or perhaps simply by the call of adventure. They brought with them knowledge, traditions, and the fundamental human drive to build communities, to understand their world, and to leave their mark.

The story of North America before 1500 is the story of these ancient peoples and their profound, intricate relationships with their environments. It's a story of deep time, of civilizations rising and adapting, of cultures flourishing in every imaginable landscape. To truly understand this continent and the peoples who first inhabited it, we must begin by appreciating the sheer diversity of its lands and the equally diverse tapestry of human cultures that called it home for so long. It is a prelude to understanding not just who these people were, but how they lived, what they believed, and the incredible legacy they created long before any outsiders ever set foot on their shores. This immense geographical canvas is the backdrop against which the rich and varied stories of North America's First Peoples unfolded.

The sheer scale of North America before 1500 CE is almost unfathomable. It was a continent of dramatic contrasts, a land shaped by powerful natural forces over millions of years, and subsequently, by the ingenuity and resilience of its human inhabitants for thousands of years. Imagine standing on the edge of the Arctic tundra, the wind whipping across a vast, treeless expanse where the ground is frozen for most of the year. Here, life was a testament to survival, with communities like the Inuit developing an intimate understanding of the ice, the sea, and the migratory patterns of the animals that provided their sustenance. Their world was one of stark beauty, where the aurora borealis painted the night sky and the long days of summer brought a brief, intense burst of life.

Venture south, and the landscape shifts dramatically. The Eastern Woodlands, a region characterized by dense forests, rolling hills, and abundant waterways like the Great Lakes and the mighty Mississippi, became home to a multitude of diverse peoples. These forests were not simply trees; they were a living pantry and a boundless source of building materials. Oak, maple, hickory, and pine provided not only shelter and tools but also acorns, nuts, and maple sap that were essential parts of the diet. Rivers and lakes teemed with fish – salmon, trout, bass – while the forests themselves offered game such as deer, bear, rabbit, and turkey. This environment fostered the development of settled agricultural communities, particularly along the fertile river valleys, where crops like corn, beans, and squash – the "Three Sisters" – were cultivated, forming the cornerstone of many diets. Yet, hunting and fishing remained vital, and the ability to navigate these complex waterways by canoe was a crucial skill.

Further west, the landscape opens up into the immense expanse of the Great Plains. This is a realm defined by grass, stretching as far as the eye can see, a sea of green and gold that swayed with the slightest breeze. For much of this region, the bison was king. These massive herbivores, numbering in the tens of millions, were not just a food source; they were the very foundation of life for the nomadic peoples who followed them. Every part of the bison was utilized: the meat for food, the hides for clothing and shelter (the iconic tipi), the bones for tools and weapons, the sinew for thread. Life on the Plains was dictated by the movements of the herds and the changing seasons, requiring a deep knowledge of the land, weather patterns, and the behavior of these magnificent animals.

Moving southwest, the environment becomes significantly more challenging. The deserts of Arizona, New Mexico, and parts of Utah and Colorado are characterized by extreme temperatures, scarce water, and rugged terrain. Yet, life here is anything but barren. Indigenous peoples of the Southwest, such as the ancestors of the Pueblo, Hopi, and Zuni, became masters of adaptation. They developed sophisticated agricultural techniques, including intricate irrigation systems to channel precious water to their crops and dry-farming methods to capture moisture from infrequent rains. Their architectural achievements are legendary, from the multi-story adobe pueblos that still stand today to the astonishing cliff dwellings built into the sides of canyons, offering both shelter and defense. These communities carved out a rich cultural existence in a demanding landscape, their lives interwoven with the cycles of the sun, the stars, and the scarce but vital water sources.

Along the vast Pacific coast, from what is now Alaska down to California, a different abundance prevailed. Here, the Pacific Ocean provided a seemingly inexhaustible supply of fish, shellfish, and marine mammals. Towering cedar forests, nourished by plentiful rainfall, offered a rich source of wood for building sturdy homes, crafting intricate canoes capable of navigating the open ocean, and carving elaborate totem poles and ceremonial objects. The peoples of this region, such as the Kwakwaka'wakw, Haida, and Coast Salish, developed complex social structures often centered around lineage and the accumulation of wealth, famously expressed through the potlatch ceremony. Their lives were deeply connected to the rhythms of the sea and the forest, a testament to living in harmony with a land of plenty.

Even beyond these broad regions, the diversity continued. The Rocky Mountains presented another distinct environment, a high-altitude world of rugged peaks, deep valleys, and alpine meadows. Peoples like the Shoshone and Ute adapted to this challenging terrain, utilizing its resources for hunting and gathering, and often moving seasonally between different elevations. The Great Basin, a vast arid region between the Rockies and the Sierra Nevada, presented its own set of challenges, fostering a more nomadic lifestyle focused on hunting small game and gathering seeds, nuts, and roots.

This immense geographical diversity was not merely a passive backdrop; it actively shaped the lives, cultures, and societies of the Indigenous peoples of North America. The resources available dictated the types of food people ate, the materials they used for shelter and tools, and even the ways they organized themselves socially and politically. The very worldview of a people was often deeply intertwined with the specific environment they inhabited – the spirits of the animals they hunted, the power of the mountains they revered, the life-giving properties of the rivers they depended on.

Furthermore, it's crucial to remember that human presence on this continent stretched back millennia. Archaeological evidence, combined with rich oral traditions passed down through generations, speaks to a deep history of human adaptation, innovation, and cultural development. These weren't newly arrived people; they were the inheritors of ancient wisdom, their ancestors having navigated periods of dramatic climate change, the arrival and departure of ice sheets, and the gradual shaping of the landscapes we see today. This long tenure on the land fostered an unparalleled understanding of its ecosystems, its cycles, and its possibilities.

Therefore, before 1500, North America was not a blank slate. It was a continent already densely populated, culturally rich, and geographically varied. It was a land of many nations, each with its own distinct identity, its own history, and its own sophisticated relationship with the environment. Understanding this vast and ancient land, in all its magnificent diversity, is the essential first step in appreciating the incredible tapestry of Indigenous cultures that flourished across it for thousands of years. This pre-contact world was one of immense human achievement, setting the stage for the complex interactions that would eventually unfold. The continent itself was a character in the story, a powerful force that shaped and was shaped by the peoples who called it home. Its mountains, forests, plains, rivers, and coastlines were not just features on a map, but living entities that held spiritual significance, provided essential resources, and dictated the rhythms of daily life for countless generations. This deep and enduring connection between people and place is a central theme in understanding the history of North America before the arrival of Europeans.

2 | The First Peoples and Their Homes

The story of human presence in North America stretches back into an unfathomable past, a tapestry woven with threads of migration, adaptation, and profound connection to the land. Long before any written records, for tens of thousands of years, people journeyed across this vast continent, each step guided by survival, curiosity, and an innate drive to build a life. These were not fleeting visits, but the beginnings of enduring cultures, each finding its unique niche in the diverse environments that North America offered. The earliest chapters of this human story are often pieced together through the careful work of archaeologists, who unearth the remnants of ancient camps, tools, and hearths, and through the powerful oral traditions passed down through countless generations of Indigenous peoples, stories that carry the wisdom and experiences of their ancestors.

The initial peopling of North America is a subject of ongoing scientific exploration, but a leading theory suggests that early peoples migrated from Asia, likely across a land bridge that once connected Siberia and Alaska during a period of lower sea levels, perhaps as long as 20,000 years ago or even earlier. These were not organized armies on a conquest, but rather small, mobile groups following the abundant game animals that roamed the glacial landscapes. Imagine these intrepid explorers, moving across vast, open territories, their knowledge of the environment their most crucial tool. They learned to read the subtle signs of the seasons, the habits of migrating herds, and the locations of essential water sources. The tools they fashioned – carefully chipped stone points for spears, scrapers for hides, and grinding stones for seeds – are testaments to their ingenuity and their deep understanding of the materials available to them.

As the great ice sheets that once covered much of the continent began to recede, opening new territories, these early peoples spread out. Their movements were not random; they were strategic journeys into regions that offered promise for sustenance and shelter. Some groups ventured south, encountering a dramatically different North America than the icy expanse they had left behind. Others moved eastward, finding themselves in the burgeoning forests and river systems of what would become known as the Eastern Woodlands. The sheer diversity of the continent provided an incredible array of ecological niches, each presenting unique challenges and opportunities that would shape the development of distinct ways of life.

Consider the incredible adaptability required to thrive in these early, often challenging, environments. In regions that would later become arid, ancient peoples learned to harvest the sparse but vital resources. They became adept at identifying edible desert plants, seeds, and roots, and in some areas, developed techniques for collecting and storing precious water. The archaeological record in these areas reveals sophisticated tools for processing tough plant materials and evidence of seasonal movements to exploit different food sources throughout the year. Oral traditions from these regions often speak of a deep reverence for the earth and its limited bounty, and of the wisdom passed down to understand and respect the delicate balance of life in arid lands.

Moving into the vast forested regions, early inhabitants found a world teeming with life. The dense woodlands offered abundant game – deer, elk, smaller mammals – and a rich variety of plant life. Rivers and lakes provided fish and a means of travel. Here, communities likely began to establish more settled patterns, utilizing the readily available resources for food, shelter, and tools. The construction of simple dwellings, perhaps made from branches, leaves, and animal hides, would have provided protection from the elements. Evidence of early fishing techniques, such as the use of nets and traps, and hunting strategies, are found in the archaeological sites of these areas, painting a picture of people living in close harmony with their woodland surroundings.

The expansion across North America was not a single, swift event, but a long, drawn-out process, spanning millennia. As these early populations encountered new environments, they didn't simply survive; they innovated. They developed new technologies, refined their hunting and gathering techniques, and began to experiment with cultivating certain plants. The development of agriculture, a transformative shift in human history, occurred independently in various parts of the world, and North America was no exception. While the exact timing and origins of agriculture in the Americas are complex, it's clear that Indigenous peoples across the continent, over vast stretches of time, began to cultivate crops like maize (corn), beans, and squash, which would profoundly alter their societies.

The development of settled life and agriculture allowed for greater population densities and the emergence of more complex social structures. In some regions, the surplus of food could support individuals who weren't directly involved in food production, leading to specialization in crafts, leadership, and spiritual practices. This gradual process of adaptation and innovation laid the foundation for the diverse and sophisticated cultures that would flourish across North America for thousands of years. The ability to thrive in such a wide range of environments, from the icy north to the arid southwest, from the eastern forests to the western coasts, speaks to the remarkable resilience, ingenuity, and deep knowledge of the land possessed by the First Peoples of this continent. Their story is one of continuity, of people not just occupying the land, but becoming an integral part of its unfolding natural and cultural history, a testament to the enduring power of human adaptation and innovation.

The journey of the First Peoples across North America was a testament to their profound understanding of the natural world and their incredible capacity for adaptation. These were not static populations, but dynamic groups constantly interacting with and responding to their surroundings. As they moved from the initial entry points, perhaps through the glacial refugia of Beringia or along the Pacific coast, they encountered a continent of staggering environmental diversity. Each new landscape presented a unique set of challenges and opportunities, and over thousands of years, distinct ways of life emerged, tailored to the specific resources and conditions of each region.

In the far north, the Arctic environment presented an extreme test of human endurance. Here, the Inuit and their ancestors developed an intimate relationship with the ice and snow. Their survival depended on a deep knowledge of sea ice formation, the migratory patterns of seals, walruses, and whales, and the habits of caribou on the tundra. Their ingenious shelters, such as the snow house or *igloo*, were marvels of engineering, perfectly adapted to the frigid conditions, providing warmth and protection from the harsh winds. Their tools, crafted from bone, ivory, and stone, were remarkably efficient for hunting, fishing, and processing animal hides, which provided their clothing and shelter. The vastness of the Arctic, with its long periods of darkness and its brief, intense summers, shaped their worldview, fostering a deep respect for the elements and the interconnectedness of all life. Oral traditions from this region often speak of a spiritual connection to the animals that sustained them, recognizing the reciprocal relationship between hunter and prey.

Venturing south into the boreal forests and the temperate woodlands of eastern North America, early peoples encountered a different, yet equally demanding, environment. The abundance of trees provided readily available materials for building more permanent shelters, such as longhouses or wigwams, and for crafting canoes that allowed them to navigate the extensive network of rivers, lakes, and coastal waterways. The forests teemed with game animals like deer, bear, and rabbit, and the waterways offered a rich harvest of fish and waterfowl. In many of these areas, a gradual shift towards agriculture began, with the cultivation of maize, beans, and squash – the "Three Sisters" – becoming increasingly important. This agricultural revolution allowed for more settled communities, the development of villages, and the potential for food surpluses. The archaeological record in these regions shows evidence of sophisticated village planning, burial practices, and the development of pottery for cooking and storage. The stories of these peoples often emphasize the importance of community, the cycles of the forest, and the wisdom of the elders.

As the landscape opened into the Great Plains, a vast, treeless expanse dominated by grasses, life took on a more nomadic character for many groups. The sheer abundance of bison, numbering in the millions, dictated the rhythm of life. These peoples became expert hunters, following the great herds across the plains. Every part of the bison was utilized: the meat for sustenance, the hides for clothing and the iconic conical dwelling known as the tipi, the bones for tools, and even the sinew for thread. The tipi, easily dismantled and transported, was perfectly suited for a mobile lifestyle. The Plains peoples developed an extraordinary understanding of the land, the weather patterns, and the behavior of the bison, their lives intricately interwoven with the cycles of these magnificent animals. Their oral traditions often speak of the freedom of the open plains, the power of the thunder, and the spiritual significance of the bison.

Further west, the environment transformed into the rugged and often arid landscapes of the Southwest. Here, the ancestors of the Pueblo, Hopi, and Zuni peoples demonstrated an incredible mastery of arid-land agriculture. They developed sophisticated irrigation systems, channeling precious water from rivers and springs to their crops of corn, beans, and squash. They also practiced dry-farming techniques, designed to capture and retain moisture from infrequent rainfall. Their architectural achievements are legendary, from the multi-story adobe pueblos, built from sun-dried mud bricks, that still stand today as impressive examples of communal living, to the breathtaking cliff dwellings, constructed within natural alcoves in canyon walls, which offered protection from the elements and from potential enemies. These peoples developed complex social and religious systems, deeply connected to the cycles of the sun, the stars, and the vital water sources that sustained them. Their stories often recount the journeys of their ancestors, their deep connection to the earth, and the spiritual significance of the landscape.

The Pacific coast, with its temperate rainforests and abundant marine life, offered yet another rich tapestry of resources. The peoples of this region, such as the ancestors of the Kwakwaka'wakw, Haida, and Coast Salish, benefited from the bounty of the ocean – salmon, cod, halibut, shellfish – and the towering cedar forests. Cedar wood was essential for building sturdy, large plank houses, for crafting magnificent ocean-going canoes capable of long voyages, and for creating intricate artwork, including the renowned totem poles. These societies often developed complex social hierarchies, with wealth and status playing significant roles, often expressed through elaborate ceremonies like the potlatch. Their lives were intimately tied to the rhythms of the tides and the bounty of the sea, and their stories frequently speak of the power of the ocean, the spirits of the forest, and the importance of lineage.

Beyond these broad regional patterns, countless other environments fostered unique adaptations. The mountainous regions of the Rockies, for instance, were home to peoples like the Shoshone and Ute, who skillfully navigated the high altitudes, hunting game and gathering plants that thrived in alpine meadows. Their seasonal movements between different elevations allowed them to exploit a variety of resources throughout the year. In the Great Basin, a vast arid region between the Sierra Nevada and the Rocky Mountains, life was often more nomadic, with groups expertly gathering seeds, nuts, roots, and small game, their knowledge of the land and its subtle resources paramount to their survival.

The continuity of human presence on this continent is a profound aspect of this early history. For thousands of years, these peoples lived, learned, and passed down their knowledge. They experienced climate changes, the evolution of landscapes, and the gradual development of their own unique cultural traditions. The archaeological evidence, combined with the rich oral histories, paints a picture of continuous adaptation and innovation, a testament to the enduring resilience of Indigenous peoples. They were not passive inhabitants of a pristine wilderness, but active stewards and shapers of the land, developing a deep, reciprocal relationship with their environments that sustained them for millennia. This long tenure fostered an unparalleled understanding of ecological systems, a deep spiritual connection to the land, and the development of sophisticated knowledge systems that are still being uncovered and understood today. The diversity of these early settlements, from ephemeral hunting camps to substantial agricultural villages and impressive architectural marvels, underscores the remarkable success of the First Peoples in establishing enduring and vibrant societies across the vast and varied landscapes of North America.

3 | Diverse Ways of Living

The vast expanse of North America, stretching from the frozen shores of the Arctic to the sun-baked deserts of the Southwest, and from the Atlantic to the Pacific, was not a monolithic landscape. Instead, it was a continent of staggering diversity, a mosaic of environments that profoundly shaped the lives of the Indigenous peoples who called it home. To speak of a single "Native American way of life" before 1500 would be a disservice to the intricate tapestry of cultures that flourished across this land. Instead, we find a breathtaking spectrum of human ingenuity and adaptation, each group developing unique strategies for survival, sustenance, and societal organization, dictated by the specific resources and challenges of their homelands.

In many regions, particularly in areas with abundant game and less arable land, **hunter-gatherer societies** formed the bedrock of existence. These were peoples who lived in intimate communion with the natural world, their lives dictated by the seasonal movements of animals and the availability of wild plants. Their knowledge of the environment was encyclopedic, encompassing the habits of every creature, the edible and medicinal properties of countless plants, and the subtle signs that heralded changes in weather or the turning of the seasons. For instance, on the Great Plains, the bison was the central pillar of life for many groups. Their nomadic existence revolved around following the colossal herds, a practice that required incredible skill in tracking, hunting, and processing the animals. Every part of the bison was utilized with remarkable efficiency: the meat was a primary food source, the thick hides were tanned and fashioned into durable clothing, footwear, and the iconic, easily transportable *tipi* dwellings. Bones were transformed into tools, weapons, and even needles for sewing, while sinew provided strong thread. These Plains cultures, while nomadic, were far from simple; they possessed complex social structures, intricate spiritual beliefs interwoven with the natural world, and rich oral traditions that preserved their history and knowledge. Their shelters, the *tipis*, were engineering marvels, designed for rapid erection and dismantling, perfectly suited for a life on the move, offering warmth and protection against the often harsh prairie winds.

In contrast, other regions witnessed the rise of **agricultural communities**, where the cultivation of crops became a cornerstone of their societies. This shift, a profound transformation in human history, allowed for more settled lifestyles, the development of larger villages, and the potential for food surpluses that could support populations year-round. In the fertile river valleys of the Eastern Woodlands, for example, peoples like those of the Mississippian culture developed sophisticated agricultural practices, with maize (corn), beans, and squash – the "Three Sisters" – forming the basis of their diet. These crops were often grown together, with the beans

providing nitrogen to the soil, the corn stalks offering support for the climbing beans, and the squash vines spreading to shade the ground, suppressing weeds and retaining moisture. This symbiotic relationship not only improved crop yields but also created a highly nutritious and balanced diet. These communities often lived in more permanent villages, with substantial houses and often organized around ceremonial centers. The emergence of agriculture allowed for the specialization of labor; not everyone needed to be directly involved in food production, leading to the development of skilled artisans, builders, spiritual leaders, and administrators. Their shelters varied, from the large, communal *longhouses* to smaller *wigwams*, constructed from materials like wood, bark, and animal hides, reflecting the abundant resources of the forested environment. The archaeological record reveals evidence of planned settlements, with plazas, mounds, and defensive palisades, indicating a high degree of social organization and cooperation.

Along the vast and bountiful coastlines, a third distinct way of life emerged: **coastal fishing villages**. Peoples living along the Pacific coast, for instance, from the temperate rainforests of the Northwest to the more arid coasts of California, developed livelihoods deeply intertwined with the sea and its abundant resources. The ocean offered a consistent and rich source of food, including a wide array of fish like salmon, cod, and halibut, as well as shellfish, seals, and whales. Salmon, in particular, played a vital role in the diet and economy of many Northwest Coast cultures, with elaborate methods for catching, preserving, and storing the fish to last through leaner times. These communities often lived in permanent villages, building sturdy homes from the readily available cedar timber. The towering cedar trees of the Pacific Northwest were not just building materials; they were central to every aspect of life, used to construct large, seaworthy canoes capable of long voyages, to carve intricate artwork, and to create the renowned totem poles that depicted lineage, stories, and spiritual beliefs. Their social structures were often complex, with an emphasis on lineage, social status, and elaborate ceremonial practices, such as the *potlatch*, where wealth was distributed to demonstrate status and solidify social bonds.

Even within these broad categories, immense variation existed, dictated by local geography and resource availability. In the arid Southwest, for example, peoples like the ancestors of the Pueblo, Hopi, and Zuni developed remarkable adaptations for desert living. Their reliance on agriculture, particularly maize, demanded extraordinary ingenuity in water management. They engineered sophisticated irrigation systems, channeling precious water from rivers and springs to their fields, and developed dry-farming techniques to capture and conserve moisture from the infrequent rainfall. Their architectural achievements are legendary, from the multi-story *pueblos* – communities built from sun-dried mud bricks, or *adobe*, that still stand today as testaments to communal living – to the breathtaking *cliff dwellings* constructed within natural alcoves in canyon walls, offering both protection and a deep connection to the landscape.

The diversity of shelters across North America was as varied as the environments themselves. Beyond the *tipis* of the Plains, the *longhouses* and *wigwams* of the Woodlands, and the *pueblos* and cliff dwellings of the Southwest, consider the subterranean dwellings of some Arctic peoples, offering insulation against extreme cold, or the woven mat houses of some California groups, adapted to milder climates. Similarly, tools and clothing were meticulously crafted from the materials at hand. Bone, stone, and wood were fashioned into knives, projectile points, scrapers, grinding stones, and weaving implements. Clothing varied from the thick, fur-lined garments of Arctic peoples, essential for survival in sub-zero temperatures, to the lighter, woven fabrics of warmer regions, or the tanned hides of deer and bison used by many groups.

The clothing of many Indigenous peoples was not merely functional; it was also a form of cultural expression, adorned with intricate beadwork, quillwork, or painted designs that held symbolic meaning and conveyed identity. The tools, too, reflected a deep understanding of materials and their properties. The finely flaked obsidian points of the Southwest, the polished stone axes of the Northeast, and the bone needles used for sewing by Arctic peoples all demonstrate a sophisticated level of craftsmanship honed over millennia.

This mosaic of lifestyles – hunter-gatherers following game, farmers cultivating the land, fishers harvesting the sea, and ingenious desert dwellers mastering arid environments – highlights a crucial point: there was no single "Native American" experience before 1500. Instead, there was a continent teeming with diverse nations, each with its own unique history, language, social structures, spiritual beliefs, and, importantly, distinct ways of life. Their adaptations were not merely reactive; they were proactive, innovative responses to the challenges and opportunities presented by the North American continent. These diverse societies, each a testament to human resilience and creativity, laid the groundwork for the complex and vibrant cultures that would continue to evolve and interact for centuries to come.

4 | Connection to the Natural World

The Indigenous peoples of North America before 1500 did not merely *live* on the land; they were an intrinsic part of it, their lives, beliefs, and survival inextricably woven into the fabric of the natural world. This was not a passive coexistence but a dynamic, reciprocal relationship built on profound understanding, deep respect, and a philosophy of stewardship. Every aspect of their existence—from the food they ate and the shelters they built to the stories they told and the ceremonies they performed—was informed by an encyclopedic knowledge of the environment. This intimate connection fostered a worldview centered on interconnectedness, a stark contrast to the more utilitarian and exploitative approach that would later characterize European colonization.

Their understanding of plants, for instance, went far beyond simple identification for food or medicine, though these were vital. They understood the life cycles of flora, knowing when and where to harvest roots, berries, nuts, and leaves to ensure future abundance. They recognized the medicinal properties of countless plants, utilizing them to heal ailments, from minor cuts and fevers to more serious conditions. Certain plants held spiritual significance, appearing in origin stories, ceremonies, and as symbols of particular clans or peoples. The careful, selective harvesting of plants was a practice rooted in the principle of reciprocity; taking only what was needed and ensuring that the plant populations could regenerate was seen as a sacred duty. This ensured the long-term health of both the ecosystems and the communities that depended on them. For example, the gathering of wild rice by Anishinaabeg peoples in the Great Lakes region was a meticulously managed process. They understood the specific water conditions needed for the wild rice to flourish and harvested it with specialized tools that allowed them to dislodge the grains without damaging the stalks, ensuring a bountiful harvest for generations to come. The very act of gathering was often accompanied by prayers and offerings of gratitude to the plant spirits.

Similarly, the relationship with animals was one of profound respect and understanding. Indigenous hunters possessed an intimate knowledge of animal behavior, migration patterns, and the subtle signs that indicated their presence or mood. Hunting was not simply about acquiring meat or hides; it was a spiritual undertaking. Before embarking on a hunt, hunters would often engage in purification rituals, offer prayers, and seek guidance from spiritual leaders or elders. When an animal was taken, it was treated with reverence. Every part of the animal was used, minimizing waste and honoring the sacrifice. The Plains peoples' relationship with the bison exemplifies this. As previously noted, the bison provided sustenance, shelter, and tools. Beyond the practical, the bison was a central figure in many Plains creation stories and spiritual beliefs, often seen as a gift from the Creator. The act of hunting the bison was imbued with ceremony, and the successful hunt was a cause for communal celebration and gratitude. Rituals surrounding the prepara-tion of the hide, the sharing of the meat, and the crafting of tools from bone and horn all underscored the deep respect for the animal that had provided so much. This was not a relationship of dominion, but of kinship.

The cycles of nature—the changing seasons, the movements of the sun, moon, and stars—were not merely observed but deeply understood and integrated into the rhythm of daily life and spiritual practice. Astronomical knowledge was sophisticated, used for navigation, agriculture, and the timing of ceremonies. The solstices and equinoxes, for instance, were often marked by significant gatherings and rituals, acknowledging the Earth's turning and the celestial powers that governed it. Many Indigenous cultures had intricate calendars based on lunar cycles or the position of stars, which guided agricultural planting, hunting expeditions, and important ceremonies. The Anasazi peoples of the Southwest, for instance, meticulously aligned their structures, such as the Sun Temple at Mesa Verde, to track celestial events like the summer solstice, demonstrating a profound connection between their architecture, their spiritual beliefs, and the cosmos. This celestial awareness fostered a sense of cosmic order and humanity's place within it, emphasizing the interconnectedness of all things—earth, sky, and life.

Figure 1. Woodhenge at sunrise

This philosophy of interconnectedness naturally extended to the concept of reciprocity. Indigenous peoples understood that the natural world provided for them, and in turn, they had a responsibility to care for it. This was not a burden but a fundamental aspect of their worldview. They acted as stewards of the land, practicing methods that ensured sustainability. This included controlled burns to promote certain plant growth, selective harvesting, and the careful management of water resources. Their governance systems often reflected this stewardship, with decisions made by elders and councils that considered the long-term impact on the environment and future generations. There was an inherent understanding that the health of the land was directly linked to the health and well-being of the people. This principle of reciprocity meant that if they took from the land, they also gave back, whether through prayers, offerings, or actions that maintained ecological balance. For example, some coastal communities practiced a form of rotational fishing, allowing certain areas to replenish before returning to harvest them, ensuring the continued abundance of marine life.

The spiritual dimension of this relationship was paramount. The natural world was not seen as a collection of inanimate resources but as a living entity, populated by spirits and imbued with sacred power. Every mountain, river, tree, and animal was thought to possess its own spirit, and maintaining harmonious relationships with these spirits was essential for well-being. Ceremonies were often dedicated to appeasing or thanking these spirits, ensuring continued favor and balance. Origin stories and myths frequently featured animals or natural phenomena as central characters, explaining the creation of the world and humanity's place within it. These narratives served not only to transmit cultural knowledge but also to reinforce the sacredness of the natural world and the reciprocal obligations that existed between humans and their environment. The reverence for water, for example, was universal. Rivers and lakes were not just sources of sustenance but were often seen as living entities, associated with fertility, purification, and powerful spirits. Ceremonies involving water were common, seeking blessings for health, prosperity, and the continued flow of life.

This deep ecological wisdom and spiritual connection meant that Indigenous societies before 1500 lived in a state of dynamic balance with their environments. Their innovations in agriculture, hunting, and resource management were not driven by a desire for unchecked growth or accumulation, but by the need to live sustainably within the limits of their ecosystems. This philosophy of interconnectedness, respect, and reciprocity formed the bedrock of their cultures and ensured the flourishing of diverse and complex societies across the vast North American continent for millennia. It represented a profound understanding of a world where humanity was not separate from, but a vital and responsible part of, the greater web of life.

5 | Early Trade and Communication Networks

Long before the arrival of Europeans, the North American continent thrummed with the energy of extensive trade and communication networks. These were not the haphazard wanderings of isolated groups, but intricate systems of exchange and information flow that connected diverse peoples across vast distances. Goods, ideas, technologies, and spiritual practices traveled along well-worn paths, demonstrating a sophisticated level of social, economic, and cultural organization among Indigenous communities. These networks painted a picture of interconnectedness, where communities were not islands unto themselves but active participants in a continent-wide web of relationships that predated sustained European contact by millennia.

The exchange of material goods formed a significant pillar of these early networks. Essential resources, often unique to specific geographical regions, were highly valued and sought after. Obsidian, a volcanic glass prized for its sharpness and used to craft finely honed tools and weapons, is a prime example. Deposits of obsidian, such as those found at places like the Glass Buttes in Oregon or in the Jemez Mountains of New Mexico, became vital hubs in regional and even transcontinental trade. Archaeologists have traced obsidian artifacts hundreds, sometimes thousands, of miles from their geological origins, indicating the movement of this precious material through multiple hands and over extended periods. This trade was not a simple one-way transaction; it fueled a dynamic economy where prestige items, utilitarian goods, and raw materials constantly circulated.

Similarly, marine shells, particularly those from the Pacific coast and the Gulf of Mexico, found their way inland, adorning the necks and ears of people living far from any ocean. The Haliotis (abalone) shells of the Pacific coast, with their iridescent beauty, were highly prized by peoples in the interior Southwest and even as far east as the Mississippi Valley. Likewise, the distinctive shells of conch and whelk from the Gulf of Mexico traveled north and west, becoming important elements in ceremonial objects and social status markers among the peoples of the Eastern Woodlands and the Ohio River Valley. The sheer effort involved in transporting these fragile items across diverse terrains—mountains, plains, and forests—speaks volumes about their perceived value and the robustness of the transportation and exchange systems in place.

Perhaps one of the most remarkable materials exchanged was copper. While some copper deposits exist in various locations, the most significant source of native copper easily accessible to Indigenous peoples was along the southern shore of Lake Superior. From this region, expertly worked copper artifacts—axes, knives, awls, and decorative items—

traveled extensively. Evidence suggests that Lake Superior copper was traded as far south as the Gulf Coast and as far east as the Atlantic seaboard, traversing a continent-spanning network. The processing of this copper, often through hammering and annealing rather than smelting, required significant skill and knowledge, which itself could be considered a form of specialized craft knowledge that was shared or transferred through these trade routes. The existence of large, expertly crafted copper tools and ceremonial objects found in burials far from their origin point underscores the importance of this material and the sophisticated mechanisms by which it was distributed.

Beyond these high-value items, agricultural products also moved through these networks. While many communities cultivated their own crops, regional specializations meant that certain foodstuffs were in demand elsewhere. For instance, maize (corn), beans, and squash, the "three sisters" that formed the agricultural backbone of many societies, were cultivated with varying degrees of success and adaptation in different climates and soil types. This led to the exchange of seeds, planting knowledge, and eventually, the surplus crops themselves. Cacao beans, native to Mesoamerica, are believed to have been traded northward into the Hohokam culture of the American Southwest, indicating connections that stretched across modern international borders. The movement of these agricultural staples not only provided dietary diversity but also supported population growth and the development of more settled communities.

The exchange of goods was intrinsically linked with the exchange of ideas, beliefs, and cultural practices. The very act of trade fostered interaction, creating opportunities for storytelling, the sharing of spiritual insights, and the dissemination of technological innovations. As traders moved between communities, they carried with them not just tangible items but also the intangible elements of their cultures. This facilitated a remarkable degree of cultural diffusion and shared understanding across the continent. Stories of creation, heroic deeds, and explanations of the natural world were passed down, adapting and evolving as they traveled. Religious ceremonies and cosmologies, while maintaining their distinct local flavors, often shared common themes and motifs, suggesting a deep well of shared spiritual understanding that transcended tribal boundaries.

For example, the widespread reverence for certain animals, such as the turtle, serpent, or bird, and their symbolic significance in creation stories and cosmology, indicates a shared intellectual and spiritual heritage. The concept of the shaman or medicine person, a spiritual intermediary who could heal, divine, and interact with the spirit world, was a common feature across many Indigenous cultures, with variations in practice and specific spiritual affiliations. The adoption and adaptation of new technologies, such as improved pottery techniques or more efficient agricultural methods, also traveled along these routes. The introduction of the bow and arrow, for instance, revolutionized hunting and warfare, and its spread across the continent was likely facilitated by these established trade and communication channels.

The physical routes themselves were a testament to the ingenuity and perseverance of Indigenous peoples. These were not simply random paths but carefully managed arteries of commerce and communication. In the East, trails like the Great Trail (or Iroquois Trail) connected communities from the St. Lawrence River to the Potomac River, facilitating the movement of goods like furs, shells, and agricultural products. In the Southwest, the Hohokam people developed extensive irrigation systems, but they also maintained trade routes that linked them to Mesoamerica, exchanging turquoise for goods like copper bells and macaw feathers. The Plains peoples, while often associated with nomadic lifestyles, also had established routes for trading bison hides, meat, and specialized tools, often following river valleys and natural landmarks.

Even coastal waters and major river systems served as highways. The Mississippi River and its tributaries formed a vast transportation network, allowing for the movement of goods and people for thousands of miles, connecting communities in the Great Lakes region with those in the Gulf of Mexico. Canoes, expertly crafted for navigating both swift rivers and open waters, were essential tools for this aquatic commerce. The reliance on these natural waterways meant that settlements often grew along riverbanks, becoming vital nodes in the larger network. Coastal communities, too, engaged in maritime trade, traveling along the coastlines to exchange fish, shells, and other marine resources.

The organization of these trade networks was complex and multifaceted. While formal markets with fixed locations and prices might not have been ubiquitous in the European sense, systems of exchange were highly structured. Gift exchange, reciprocity, and alliances played crucial roles. The act of trading was often embedded in social and political relationships. A successful trade expedition could strengthen alliances between groups, foster goodwill, and cement diplomatic ties. The reputation of traders, their reliability, and their knowledge of distant lands and peoples were valuable assets. Some individuals or families may have specialized in long-distance trade, becoming known conduits of goods and information.

The communication that accompanied this trade was equally vital. Oral traditions were the primary means of transmitting knowledge, history, and news. Stories, songs, and epic poems served not only as entertainment but as repositories of vital information about genealogies, migrations, trade routes, and ancestral lands. Messengers, often skilled runners or travelers, carried news and important messages between communities, sometimes traveling hundreds of miles. In some regions, systems of signaling, such as smoke signals or drum beats, may have been used for more immediate, albeit limited, communication across shorter distances. The intricate knowledge of geography, weather patterns, and local flora and fauna possessed by traders and travelers ensured their safe passage and facilitated their interactions with diverse groups.

The existence of these extensive trade and communication networks before 1500 fundamentally challenges the notion of Indigenous peoples as isolated and technologically backward. Instead, it reveals societies that were highly organized, socially complex, and deeply engaged in intertribal relations. These networks facilitated not only the movement of material wealth but also the vibrant exchange of knowledge, culture, and spiritual understanding, shaping a shared continental heritage that was rich and diverse. The very persistence of these networks for centuries, adapting to changing environmental conditions and the needs of different peoples, speaks to the resilience and ingenuity of Indigenous societies in North America. They were not passive inhabitants of a wild continent but active agents in shaping its cultural and economic landscape, demonstrating a level of interconnectedness and sophisticated social organization that laid the groundwork for future developments. The obsidian shards found far from their volcanic origins, the iridescent shells adorning inland burials, and the intricate copper artifacts tracing voyages across vast territories are all silent testaments to a continent alive with movement, exchange, and enduring human connection.

6 | The Eastern Woodlands: Forest Dwellers and Farmers

The Eastern Woodlands, a sprawling expanse of verdant forests, winding rivers, and a dynamic coastline, was home to a multitude of Indigenous peoples who masterfully adapted to its bountiful yet challenging environment. This region, stretching from the Atlantic Ocean to the Great Plains and from the Great Lakes down to the Gulf of Mexico, fostered diverse cultures, yet many shared common threads of ingenuity born from their forest-dwelling and farming lifestyles. Among the most prominent groups to thrive here were the Algonquian and Iroquoian language families, whose distinct societies, though varied in their specific customs, were deeply intertwined with the rhythms of the natural world.

The lives of the Eastern Woodlands peoples were intrinsically tied to the ebb and flow of the seasons. Spring brought a sense of renewal and a surge of activity. As the snow melted and the frozen earth thawed, rivers and streams teemed with returning fish, and the forests awakened with a renewed abundance of game. This was a critical time for replenishing food stores and preparing for the planting season. Many groups engaged in fishing, using sophisticated nets, traps, and spears to catch salmon, sturgeon, and a variety of other fish that migrated upstream or congregated in lakes and bays. The knowledge of fish spawning cycles and the best fishing grounds was passed down through generations, ensuring a vital source of protein.

Hunting remained a cornerstone of their subsistence, particularly in the fall and winter months when game was most plentiful and easier to track against the snow. Deer were a primary target, providing not only meat but also hides for clothing, shelter, and tools. Bears, rabbits, squirrels, and various fowl were also hunted and trapped. The development of the bow and arrow, a highly effective hunting tool, allowed for greater accuracy and efficiency. Techniques such as driving game into natural traps, ambushing them along well-worn trails, or using decoys were employed with great skill. The respect for the hunted animal was paramount, often accompanied by rituals and prayers to honor the spirit of the creature and to ensure continued success in future hunts.

While hunting and fishing provided essential sustenance, agriculture played an increasingly significant role in the lives of many Eastern Woodlands peoples, particularly those who lived in more settled communities. The cultivation of the "three sisters"—corn (maize), beans, and squash—formed the agricultural foundation of many societies. Corn, a crop that had been domesticated in Mesoamerica and gradually spread northward, became a staple, providing carbohydrates and calories. The Iroquoian peoples, in particular, were renowned for their advanced agricultural practices.

They developed methods for improving soil fertility, including the use of ashes from fires as fertilizer.

The synergy between the three sisters was a testament to their understanding of ecological principles. Corn stalks provided a natural trellis for climbing beans, while the beans, in turn, fixed nitrogen in the soil, enriching it for both corn and squash. The broad leaves of the squash plants helped to suppress weeds and retain soil moisture, creating an ideal microclimate for the other two crops. This sophisticated agricultural system allowed for the production of surplus food, which could be stored for leaner times and also supported larger, more sedentary populations.

The process of preparing and preserving food was as important as its cultivation and harvesting. Corn was often ground into flour using stone mortars and pestles, used to make various breads, porridges, and hominy. Beans were dried and stored, and squash could be dried, smoked, or stored in cool cellars. These preservation techniques were vital for surviving the long winters when fresh food was scarce. The labor of farming was often a communal effort, with men and women working together, reinforcing social bonds and shared responsibility. While men might have been more involved in hunting and clearing land, and women in planting, tending, and harvesting, these roles were often fluid and interdependent.

The bounty of the forests provided not only food but also the raw materials for shelter and tools. Wood was essential for constructing dwellings, crafting canoes, and fashioning tools and weapons. Different types of trees were favored for specific purposes; for example, sturdy hardwoods were used for building, while lighter woods were used for bows and arrows. Bark, particularly from birch and elm trees, was used to cover wigwams and to construct waterproof containers and canoes.

The iconic longhouses of the Iroquoian peoples, stretching perhaps hundreds of feet in length, were remarkable feats of engineering and community living. Built from sturdy wooden frames and covered with bark, these communal dwellings housed several families, often related through the maternal line. Each longhouse contained individual living quarters arranged along a central aisle, with hearths for cooking and heating spaced throughout. This communal living fostered a strong sense of kinship and collective identity, with decisions often made through consensus within the longhouse community.

Algonquian-speaking peoples, who inhabited a wider geographic range, often lived in smaller, more mobile shelters called wigwams. These dome-shaped or conical structures were typically made from a framework of poles covered with bark, reeds, or mats. The portability of wigwams allowed for greater flexibility in movement, enabling them to follow game or relocate to areas with richer agricultural potential.

The construction and maintenance of these homes were also communal activities, reinforcing social cohesion.

Beyond food and shelter, the Eastern Woodlands provided a wealth of resources for tools, clothing, and adornment. Stone, readily available in many areas, was fashioned into axes, knives, scrapers, and projectile points. Different types of stone, such as flint and chert, were prized for their ability to be flaked into sharp edges. Bone and antler were also ingeniously utilized to create awls, needles, fishhooks, and decorative items. The craftsmanship involved in shaping these materials into functional and often aesthetically pleasing objects speaks to the deep knowledge of natural resources and the skilled hands of the artisans.

The clothing of the Eastern Woodlands peoples was primarily made from animal hides, expertly tanned and sewn. Deerskin was soft and durable, ideal for tunics, leggings, moccasins, and breechcloths. Winter clothing was often made from heavier furs to provide warmth. The decorations on clothing, using porcupine quills, beads made from shells or bone, and intricate beadwork, served not only as adornment but also as a form of storytelling, often depicting clan symbols, spiritual beliefs, or significant life events.

The social and political structures of the Eastern Woodlands peoples were as diverse as their environments, yet kinship, community, and diplomacy were central to their organization. For the Iroquoian peoples, society was largely matrilineal, with lineage and inheritance traced through the mother's line. Clan systems were paramount, with individuals belonging to specific clans that extended across multiple villages. These clans served to regulate marriage, provide mutual support, and ensure social order. The famous Iroquois Confederacy, a powerful alliance of five (later six) nations, exemplified their sophisticated political organization. This confederacy, formed through consensus and diplomacy, provided a framework for inter-tribal relations, conflict resolution, and collective defense, showcasing an advanced form of governance that was ahead of its time.

Algonquian-speaking groups often had more decentralized political structures, with leadership typically held by chiefs or sachems whose authority was often based on persuasion, generosity, and demonstrated wisdom rather than absolute power. Decisions were often made through councils of elders or through consensus among the community. While individual tribes or bands might have been autonomous, alliances and confederacies also existed, particularly in response to external threats or for the purpose of facilitating trade and defense.

The importance of spiritual beliefs permeated all aspects of life in the Eastern Woodlands. The natural world was seen as imbued with spirit, and a deep reverence for the Creator and the forces of nature guided their actions. The interconnectedness of all living things was a central tenet, and ceremonies and rituals were performed to maintain balance and harmony with the spiritual realm. Shamans or medicine people played crucial roles as healers, spiritual guides, and intermediaries between the human and spirit worlds. Their knowledge of medicinal plants, their understanding of spiritual forces, and their ability to perform healing rituals were vital to the well-being of their communities.

The storytelling tradition was a powerful vehicle for transmitting cultural knowledge, spiritual beliefs, and historical accounts. Myths, legends, and epic tales recounted the creation of the world, the exploits of heroic ancestors, and the origins of their customs and laws. These stories were not merely entertainment; they were essential educational tools that reinforced cultural values, explained the natural world, and provided a sense of shared identity and history.

The trade networks that connected the Eastern Woodlands with other regions, as previously discussed, also played a significant role in shaping these cultures. The exchange of goods like shells, copper, and furs facilitated economic prosperity and social interaction. However, it was not just material goods that were exchanged. Ideas, stories, religious practices, and technological innovations also traveled along these routes, enriching the cultural tapestry of the region and demonstrating the interconnectedness of Indigenous peoples across the continent. The Eastern Woodlands, with its dense forests, fertile river valleys, and coastal access, provided a rich and sustaining environment for the diverse and ingenious peoples who called it home, shaping a legacy of adaptation, community, and profound connection to the land.

7 | The Mississippian Culture: Cities of the River Valleys

The fertile river valleys of the Mississippi, Ohio, and Missouri rivers witnessed the rise of one of North America's most remarkable and complex Indigenous civilizations: the Mississippian culture. Flourishing roughly between 800 and 1600 CE, this society was characterized by its large, organized populations, impressive architectural feats, sophisticated agricultural practices, and a rich spiritual and artistic life. Unlike many of their contemporaries who relied on more mobile lifestyles or smaller settlements, Mississippian peoples established enduring, densely populated centers that served as hubs of political, economic, and religious activity. These were not mere villages, but true cities, each with its own distinct character yet sharing a common cultural thread that bound them together.

At the heart of the Mississippian world lay the concept of the paramount chiefdom, a hierarchical political structure that consolidated power in the hands of a ruling elite. These chiefs, often believed to possess spiritual authority as well as secular power, oversaw vast territories and populations. Their authority was maintained through a combination of kinship ties, religious ideology, and the control of resources and labor. This system allowed for the mobilization of large workforces needed for monumental construction projects and the organization of extensive agricultural endeavors that sustained these burgeoning urban centers. The very landscape of the river valleys was transformed by their presence, as they reshaped the earth to suit their societal needs and express their worldview.

The most striking testament to Mississippian ingenuity and organizational prowess is their monumental mound-building. These earthworks, constructed over generations through the laborious process of hauling and piling soil basketful by basketful, served a variety of purposes. The most prominent were the large, flat-topped platform mounds, which often supported important public buildings such as temples or the residences of chiefs. These structures, elevated above the surrounding settlements, visually symbolized the elevated status of the ruling elite and served as focal points for public ceremonies and rituals. The sheer scale of these mounds, some rising over 100 feet in height and covering many acres at their base, is staggering and speaks volumes about the coordinated labor and societal dedication required for their construction. Sites like Monks Mound at Cahokia, the largest pre-Columbian earthwork in the Americas, exemplify this architectural grandeur. It is estimated that it took millions of basket loads of earth, moved over centuries, to create this single massive structure. The construction of such mounds was not merely an engineering feat; it was a sacred act, imbued with spiritual meaning and integral to the Mississippian cosmology.

Beyond the imposing platform mounds, Mississippians also constructed other types of earthworks, including conical burial mounds, ridge-top mounds, and even animal-shaped effigy mounds, particularly in the western reaches of their influence.

The burial mounds, often containing the remains of individuals of high status accompanied by elaborate grave goods, provide invaluable insights into their social stratification and beliefs about the afterlife. The careful curation of these burial sites underscores the importance of lineage and the veneration of ancestors within Mississippian society. The effigy mounds, often depicting animals such as panthers, birds, or serpents, suggest a deep connection to the animal world and likely played a role in their spiritual practices and shamanistic traditions.

The sustenance for these large populations was provided by an advanced and highly productive agricultural system, centered around the cultivation of maize (corn), beans, and squash—the "three sisters" that formed the dietary backbone of many Indigenous societies in North America. However, Mississippian farmers took this cultivation to a new level of intensity and scale. They developed sophisticated techniques for clearing and preparing large tracts of land, particularly the fertile floodplains of the major rivers. Extensive networks of ditches and canals were employed to manage water levels, ensuring optimal conditions for crop growth and preventing devastating floods. The use of hoes made from stone and shell, along with digging sticks, allowed for efficient planting and cultivation.

The surplus food produced through these intensive agricultural practices was crucial. It not only fed the growing populations of their urban centers but also supported a specialized labor force engaged in mound construction, craft production, and trade. This agricultural surplus was a cornerstone of Mississippian civilization, enabling the development of complex social structures and the maintenance of large, settled communities. The storage of this surplus was also a critical aspect of their economy, with large granaries and storage pits being a common feature of their settlements. This allowed them to weather periods of scarcity and maintain a consistent food supply throughout the year, further contributing to the stability and growth of their societies.

The social fabric of Mississippian societies was intricately woven with a pronounced social hierarchy. At the apex of this structure were the paramount chiefs and their immediate families, who wielded considerable power and prestige. Below them were the nobility or elite class, who served as administrators, religious leaders, and military commanders. This class often comprised relatives of the chief, who were entrusted with important responsibilities and enjoyed privileges such as access to finer goods and elaborate burial treatments. The vast majority of the population, however, consisted of commoners, who were primarily farmers, artisans, and laborers. While their lives were undoubtedly more arduous, they benefited from the stability, security, and cultural richness provided by the complex societal structure.

Evidence for this social stratification is abundantly found in their archaeological remains, particularly in burial contexts. The individuals buried in elaborate mounds, often accompanied by a wealth of grave goods - including finely crafted pottery, shell beads, copper ornaments, and stone tools - represent the highest echelons of Mississippian society. In contrast, burials in less elaborate sites or with fewer or no grave goods likely belonged to individuals of lower social standing. The differential treatment of the dead, from the construction of their burial mounds to the grave offerings, clearly illustrates the distinct social classes that characterized Mississippian life. This hierarchical system, while seemingly rigid, also provided a framework for social cohesion and the organization of collective endeavors.

The Mississippian world was far from isolated; it was connected by extensive and sophisticated trade networks that spanned vast distances. These networks facilitated the movement of not only essential goods but also exotic materials, ideas, and cultural practices, linking disparate communities and fostering a sense of shared identity across eastern North America. Rivers, such as the Mississippi, Ohio, and Tennessee, served as vital arteries of trade, with canoes carrying a wide array of products.

Among the most prized trade items were shell beads, particularly those crafted from the marine shells of the Gulf Coast. These beautiful and labor-intensive adornments were highly valued and are found in burials across the Mississippian world, indicating their significant cultural and economic importance. Copper, sourced from the Great Lakes region, was another crucial commodity. Mississippian artisans skillfully worked this copper, hammering it into thin sheets to create elaborate ornaments such as headdresses, bracelets, and ceremonial axes. The presence of copper artifacts in Mississippian sites, far from its source, is a clear indicator of these long-distance trade connections.

Other significant trade items included mica, a shimmering mineral often used for decorative purposes and found in Appalachian mountain deposits, and flint, a hard stone essential for crafting tools and weapons, which was quarried from various sources. The exchange of these materials not only fueled economic activity but also played a crucial role in the diffusion of Mississippian culture and ideology. For instance, the widespread distribution of Mississippian pottery styles and iconographic motifs suggests that trade routes also served as conduits for the transmission of artistic traditions and religious beliefs. This interconnectedness fostered a sense of a shared Mississippian world, even among communities separated by hundreds of miles.

The artistic expressions of the Mississippian people offer a vibrant glimpse into their worldview, aesthetics, and spiritual beliefs. Their craftsmanship in pottery, stone, shell, and copper is remarkable, characterized by a keen eye for detail and a sophisticated understanding of form and decoration. Mississippian pottery is particularly renowned for its quality and diversity, ranging from utilitarian cooking vessels to highly elaborate ceremonial pieces. Many pots were decorated with incised lines, punctations, and appliqué designs, often depicting geometric patterns, animals, or human figures.

A significant development in Mississippian art was the creation of effigy pottery, where vessels were shaped to resemble animals, birds, human heads, or mythical beings. These effigies often carried symbolic meaning, reflecting the spiritual beliefs and cosmology of the people. The famous "Spiro mounds" in Oklahoma, for example, have yielded an extraordinary collection of engraved shell gorgets, depicting scenes of warfare, ritual sacrifice, and mythological figures. These intricate carvings, made from large conch shells, are miniature masterpieces that provide invaluable insights into the complex symbolic system of the Mississippian elite.

Copper artistry reached its zenith in the intricate repoussé work and hammering techniques employed to create elaborate ceremonial regalia. Headdresses adorned with copper plaques depicting falcon warriors, or breastplates engraved with intricate designs, speak to the power and status of the individuals who wore them. The recurring motifs of the falcon, serpent, and winged being in their art are often interpreted as powerful symbols associated with shamanism, warfare, and the cosmic order.

These artistic creations were not merely decorative; they were imbued with spiritual power and served as potent symbols of authority, social status, and religious devotion.

Religion was a central and unifying force within Mississippian societies, permeating all aspects of life, from the grandest public ceremonies to the most intimate personal rituals. Their cosmology was complex, often involving a layered universe with an upper world, a middle world (the earthly realm), and a lower world. Deities and supernatural beings resided in these realms, and their influence was believed to shape human destiny. The Mississippian elite, particularly the chiefs, often served as intermediaries between the human and spiritual worlds, performing sacred rituals and ceremonies to ensure the well-being of their communities and the favor of the gods.

The large platform mounds served as stages for these important religious observances. Temples, likely constructed of wood and thatch, would have crowned these elevated structures, where priests and chiefs would conduct rites and offer sacrifices. The precise nature of these ceremonies is difficult to reconstruct fully, but archaeological evidence suggests that they often involved feasting, dancing, and the ceremonial exchange of goods. Human sacrifice, though not as widespread as in some Mesoamerican cultures, appears to have been practiced in certain Mississippian contexts, often involving captives taken in warfare.

The iconic "Birdman" motif, frequently depicted in Mississippian art, is thought to represent a powerful shaman or warrior with supernatural abilities, embodying the connection between the earthly and spiritual realms. The veneration of ancestors was also an integral part of their religious practice, with the dead being honored and appeased through elaborate burial rites and offerings. The cyclical nature of life, death, and rebirth, tied to the agricultural calendar and the rhythms of the natural world, was a fundamental aspect of their spiritual understanding. The widespread presence of similar iconography and religious themes across the Mississippian world, despite regional variations, points to a shared spiritual framework that bound these diverse communities together.

The decline of the Mississippian culture, beginning around the 14th century CE, was a complex process that likely involved a combination of factors. Environmental changes, such as shifts in climate and river courses, may have disrupted their agricultural base and led to resource scarcity. Internal social and political instability, perhaps fueled by succession disputes or growing discontent among the populace, could have weakened the centralized authority of the chiefs. Furthermore, the arrival of Europeans in the following centuries brought devastating diseases to which Indigenous populations had no immunity, leading to widespread depopulation and the eventual collapse of many large, complex societies.

However, the legacy of the Mississippian culture did not vanish with the decline of its major centers. The descendants of the Mississippian peoples continued to live in the river valleys, adapting and transforming their traditions in the face of new challenges. Their influence can be seen in the cultural practices and social structures of later Indigenous groups in the region, such as the Natchez, Choctaw, and Creek peoples. The impressive mounds that dot the landscape serve as enduring reminders of this remarkable civilization – a testament to their ingenuity, their organizational skills, and their profound connection to the land they inhabited. The study of Mississippian culture continues to reveal the depth and complexity of Indigenous societies in North America, challenging outdated notions of the continent's pre-Columbian past and highlighting the sophisticated civilizations that thrived long before European arrival. The cities of the river valleys stand as silent, yet powerful, witnesses to a vibrant and influential chapter in the human story of North America.

8 | The Southwest: Masters of Arid Lands

The Southwest, a land of breathtaking canyons, vast deserts, and towering mesas, presented a formidable challenge to its inhabitants. Unlike the lush river valleys of the Mississippian world, this region demanded a different kind of ingenuity, one rooted in deep respect for the scarce resources and a profound understanding of the delicate balance of arid ecosystems. For millennia, Indigenous peoples here, ancestors to the modern Pueblo, Hopi, and Zuni, not only survived but thrived, developing sophisticated strategies for agriculture, architecture, and community life that stand as testaments to their resilience and deep connection to their homeland.

Central to their success was a mastery of agriculture in a land where water was a precious commodity. These peoples were not simply passive recipients of what nature offered; they were active participants in shaping their environment to support life. Irrigation was not a novel concept to them, but rather a perfected art. They engineered intricate systems of canals, ditches, and reservoirs to capture and channel the infrequent rainfall and the waters of perennial streams. Along the Little Colorado River, for instance, early farmers devised ways to divert water from the river to their fields, ensuring that their crops of maize, beans, and squash received a consistent supply. In areas with less reliable surface water, they employed ingenious methods of dry farming. This involved techniques like digging small basins around plants to collect dew and rainwater, planting seeds in deeper soil where moisture lingered, and using mulch to reduce evaporation. The timing of planting was also critical, often dictated by the subtle shifts in weather patterns and the blooming of specific plants. This meticulous approach to agriculture allowed them to cultivate substantial surpluses, the foundation upon which their complex societies were built. The development of drought-resistant maize varieties, a painstaking process of selective breeding over countless generations, further enhanced their ability to farm successfully in this challenging climate. These agricultural innovations were not merely practical; they were imbued with spiritual significance, reflecting a worldview that saw the earth as a living entity to be respected and nurtured. The success of the harvest was often a communal undertaking, fostering cooperation and shared responsibility among the people.

The architectural achievements of the Southwest peoples are equally remarkable, demonstrating an intimate understanding of local materials and an extraordinary ability to create durable and functional shelters. Perhaps the most iconic examples are the cliff dwellings, such as those found at Mesa Verde National Park in Colorado. These pueblos, built into the alcoves of sheer sandstone cliffs, were not just homes; they were strategic fortresses offering protection from the elements and potential enemies. The construction itself was a marvel of engineering. Large blocks of sandstone were quarried, shaped, and

then meticulously fitted together using a mortar made from mud and straw. Wooden beams, often from ponderosa pine, were painstakingly transported to support roofs and floors. The multi-story structures, some containing hundreds of rooms, included living quarters, storage areas, and ceremonial spaces like kivas—round, subterranean chambers that served as the spiritual and social heart of the community. The placement of these dwellings, often high above the canyon floor, provided natural defense and access to limited water sources. The inhabitants developed sophisticated systems for collecting rainwater and for ascending and descending the cliffs, often using hand-and-toe holds carved directly into the rock face.

Beyond the cliff dwellings, the Southwest peoples also constructed vast, multi-story pueblos on mesa tops and canyon floors. Chaco Canyon in New Mexico, a major center of the Ancestral Puebloan culture between 850 and 1250 CE, is home to some of the most impressive examples. "Pueblo Bonito," meaning "beautiful village," is a D-shaped structure that once stood four stories high and contained over 600 rooms and 20 kivas. These pueblos were not haphazard collections of buildings but were carefully planned communities, with public spaces, plazas, and defensive walls. The construction of these massive structures required immense labor, organization, and a deep understanding of masonry. Stones were quarried and dressed with stone tools, and the precision of their stonework is still admired today. The sheer scale of these buildings, combined with their integration into the natural landscape, speaks to a sophisticated understanding of architecture and urban planning. The use of local materials, such as sandstone, adobe (mudbrick), and timber, ensured that these structures blended seamlessly with their surroundings, a testament to their philosophy of living in harmony with nature. The construction of these pueblos also reflects a highly organized social structure, capable of coordinating the efforts of many individuals over extended periods.

The spiritual lives of the Southwest peoples were as rich and intricate as their material culture. Their cosmology was deeply intertwined with the natural world, recognizing the sacredness of the sun, moon, stars, rain, and the earth itself. The kivas, with their central hearths and symbolic vent shafts, were not just architectural features but also vital centers for religious ceremony, storytelling, and the transmission of ancestral knowledge. Depictions of deities and mythological beings are found in their rock art, pottery, and textiles, offering glimpses into a complex pantheon and a belief system that emphasized balance, reciprocity, and the cyclical nature of life. The "Katsina" (or Kachina) spirits, benevolent supernatural beings who bring rain and fertility, play a central role in the religious practices of the Hopi and Zuni today, and their origins can be traced back to the ancestral traditions of the region. Ceremonies were often tied to the agricultural calendar, with elaborate dances and rituals performed to ensure good harvests and the well-being of the community. The reverence for ancestors was also a significant aspect of their spiritual life, with burials often accompanied by offerings and specific burial practices designed to honor the deceased and ensure their safe passage into the afterlife. The connection between the spiritual and the practical was paramount; every action, from planting a seed to building a home, was undertaken with a sense of sacred duty and responsibility.

The artistic expressions of the Southwest peoples are characterized by their beauty, functionality, and deep symbolic meaning. Pottery making was a highly developed art form, with distinct styles emerging across different regions and time periods. The Ancestral Puebloans, for example, are known for their exquisite black-on-white pottery, characterized by intricate geometric designs and fine-line painting. The Mimbres culture, in southwestern New Mexico, is famous for its distinctive pottery featuring realistic and often whimsical depictions of animals, humans, and mythological creatures. These vessels were not merely utilitarian objects; they were canvases for artistic expression and vehicles for storytelling. The techniques involved in pottery production were sophisticated, including the careful selection and preparation of clay, the use of natural pigments for decoration, and firing methods that produced durable and aesthetically pleasing wares.

Weaving was another crucial art form, with the Southwest peoples developing advanced techniques for spinning and weaving cotton and, in some areas, wool from domesticated animals. The resulting textiles were not only used for clothing, blankets, and ceremonial garments but also held significant symbolic and economic value. The intricate patterns and designs woven into these textiles often conveyed social status, clan affiliations, and religious beliefs. The quality of their weaving, with fine threads and complex patterns, is a testament to the skill and dedication of the weavers. The dyes used were often derived from plants and minerals found in the local environment, showcasing a deep knowledge of natural resources. The creation of these textiles was often a communal activity, with women playing a central role in the spinning, dyeing, and weaving processes. The distribution of these finely crafted goods through trade networks also played a role in fostering inter-community relationships and the exchange of cultural ideas. The continuity of these artistic traditions, from ancient times to the present day, underscores the enduring cultural heritage of the Southwest peoples. Their artistic creations serve as tangible links to their ancestors, offering a profound connection to the past and a vibrant expression of their ongoing cultural identity. The meticulous craftsmanship and profound symbolism evident in their pottery and textiles continue to inspire awe and admiration, reflecting a worldview where beauty and utility were inextricably linked.

9 | The Pacific Northwest: Bounty of the Sea and Forest

The Pacific Northwest, a region blessed with a dramatic coastline and verdant, ancient forests, fostered a way of life deeply intertwined with the bounty of both the sea and the trees. Unlike the arid Southwest, where survival demanded careful husbanding of scarce resources, the peoples of the Pacific Northwest experienced a comparative abundance. This generous environment, however, did not lead to a simpler existence; instead, it fueled a complex and rich cultural tapestry, characterized by sophisticated resource management, intricate social structures, and unparalleled artistic expression. The rhythm of life here was dictated by the ebb and flow of the tides and the steady growth of the colossal trees that dominated the landscape.

The lifeblood of the Pacific Northwest peoples was undeniably the ocean. The vast Pacific Ocean, along with the intricate network of inlets, bays, and rivers, provided an almost inexhaustible source of sustenance. Salmon, in particular, held an almost sacred status. These migratory fish, returning in massive numbers to spawn in the rivers, were a reliable and vital food source. The peoples of this region developed extraordinary skills in harvesting and preserving this aquatic bounty. Elaborate fishing techniques were employed, honed over generations of observation and practice. Long, slender spears were used to expertly pierce the swift-moving salmon in the clear river waters. Dip nets, often made from plant fibers or animal sinew, were skillfully manipulated from canoes or platforms constructed along the riverbanks, allowing for the efficient capture of large quantities of fish. Weirs, essentially intricate dams built across rivers, were designed to funnel salmon into confined areas, making them easier to catch. These weirs were not just simple barriers; they were marvels of engineering, often incorporating sophisticated traps and sluice gates to manage the flow of water and fish. The sheer scale of the salmon runs meant that not only could communities feed themselves, but they could also preserve surplus fish for leaner times. This preservation was a crucial skill, often involving smoking the salmon over slow-burning fires, which dried the fish and prevented spoilage, allowing it to be stored for extended periods. The resulting dried salmon was a staple, easily transported and providing essential protein throughout the year.

Beyond salmon, the ocean teemed with other edible resources. Halibut, cod, and various other groundfish were caught using hooks fashioned from bone, shell, or wood, often attached to long lines made from plant fibers. Shellfish, including mussels, clams, and oysters, were harvested from tidal flats and rocky shores in abundance. The rich marine environment also provided seals, sea lions, and whales, which were hunted with great skill and courage. Whaling, in particular, was a dangerous and highly respected undertaking, requiring large, seaworthy canoes and a

deep understanding of animal behavior. The successful hunt of a whale provided not only a vast amount of food but also valuable oil for lamps and a rich source of materials for tools and implements. The intertidal zones and coastal waters were a veritable supermarket, and the peoples of the Pacific Northwest possessed the knowledge and tools to expertly harvest from it. Their diet was therefore diverse and nutritious, reflecting a sophisticated understanding of the marine ecosystem and its seasonal rhythms. This intimate knowledge of the ocean's cycles, from the timing of the salmon runs to the best times for harvesting shellfish, was passed down through generations, ensuring the continued prosperity of their communities.

Equally vital to the survival and prosperity of the Pacific Northwest peoples was the forest. The towering cedar trees, with their immense size and rot-resistant wood, were a cornerstone of their material culture. Cedar was not merely a building material; it was a versatile resource that permeated every aspect of life. The outer bark of the cedar was stripped and processed into durable fibers, which were woven into a wide array of essential items. This included waterproof clothing, such as capes and hats, which were indispensable in the region's often damp climate. The fibers were also used to create strong ropes, nets for fishing and hunting, and finely woven baskets for gathering, storage, and even ceremonial purposes. The inner bark was similarly utilized for various crafts.

The majestic cedar logs themselves were transformed into the iconic dwellings and vessels of the region. Homes, known as plank houses, were constructed from massive, hand-hewn cedar planks. These structures were typically rectangular, with sturdy wooden frames and plank walls, often housing multiple families. Their size and durability allowed them to withstand the elements and provide comfortable, spacious living quarters. The construction of these plank houses was a communal effort, requiring the combined strength and skill of many individuals to fell, transport, and erect the enormous timbers. The entrance to these houses was often a large opening, sometimes framed by a carved wooden lintel. Inside, raised platforms served as sleeping areas, and a central hearth provided warmth and a place for cooking. The longevity of these cedar structures is a testament to the quality of the materials and the skill of the builders.

Perhaps the most impressive manifestation of cedar's importance was in the construction of canoes. The Pacific Northwest peoples were renowned canoe builders, crafting vessels of extraordinary size and seaworthiness from single cedar logs. These canoes, some capable of carrying fifty or more people and vast quantities of goods, were the highways of the region. They were used for fishing, hunting, warfare, and extensive trade expeditions that stretched for hundreds of miles along the coast and up the rivers. The process of creating a dugout canoe was labor-intensive and required specialized knowledge. A suitable cedar log was selected, often a massive specimen, and then hollowed out using a combination of fire and stone or shell tools. The hull was carefully shaped to ensure stability and speed, and the gunwales were often flared outwards to increase buoyancy and capacity. The resulting canoes were not merely utilitarian objects; they were works of art, often decorated with intricate carvings and painted designs that reflected the owner's status and lineage. The ability to build and navigate these sophisticated watercraft was essential for the economic and social life of the Pacific Northwest peoples, enabling them to exploit the rich resources of their environment and maintain connections with distant communities.

Beyond practical applications, cedar wood was also the medium for one of the most distinctive art forms of the Pacific Northwest: the totem pole. These monumental carvings, often towering thirty feet or more, were not idols or objects of worship in the Western sense. Instead, they served as powerful visual narratives, recording lineage, significant events, and the crests of important families. Each figure carved onto a totem pole represented a story, an ancestor, or a supernatural being associated with the family or clan. The crests, often animals such as the raven, eagle, bear, or wolf, were inherited symbols that identified individuals and groups. Totem poles were erected in front of houses, at village entrances, or to commemorate important occasions like a chief's death or the completion of a significant undertaking. The creation of a totem pole was a highly skilled and time-consuming endeavor, often commissioned by a wealthy chief and carved by master artisans. The intricate designs, the bold lines, and the vibrant colors (derived from natural pigments like ochre, charcoal, and various plant dyes) made these poles striking landmarks, communicating a wealth of information to those who understood their symbolic language. They were a public declaration of status, history, and cultural identity.

The social structures of the Pacific Northwest were as elaborate as their material culture. Wealth and status played a central role, and these were often displayed and redistributed through a unique institution known as the potlatch. The potlatch was a complex ceremony, often lasting for days, during which a host would invite guests from other communities to witness and participate in significant events. These events could include the naming of children, the raising of a totem pole, a marriage, or the passing of hereditary titles. The primary purpose of the potlatch was for the host to publicly demonstrate their wealth and prestige, but this was achieved through a seemingly paradoxical act: the giving away and often the destruction of vast quantities of property. Food, blankets, canoes, slaves, and other valuable items were distributed among the guests. The more a host gave away, the greater their prestige. Guests, in turn, were expected to reciprocate at a later date, often with interest. This system of competitive gift-giving served several important social functions. It was a mechanism for accumulating and redistributing wealth, ensuring that resources were shared throughout the region and preventing any single individual or group from hoarding too much. It also solidified alliances between communities, reinforced social hierarchies, and legitimized claims to titles and status. The more elaborate and costly a potlatch, the higher the host's standing in the community and the greater their influence. The elaborate feasts, the performances of dancers and orators, and the distribution of gifts all contributed to a vibrant and dynamic social order. This system of prestige and reciprocal obligation was fundamental to the political and economic organization of Pacific Northwest societies.

The artistic traditions of the Pacific Northwest are renowned for their distinctive style and masterful craftsmanship. The visual arts were deeply integrated with the social and spiritual lives of the people. While wood carving, particularly in cedar, was paramount, other art forms also flourished. Weaving, especially by the women of the region, produced a variety of beautiful and functional textiles. Blankets, known as Chilkat blankets, made from the wool of mountain goats and the inner bark of cedar, were particularly prized. These blankets were not only warm and durable but also adorned with intricate, colorful designs that mirrored the motifs found on totem poles and other carvings. The weaving process was complex, involving spinning the fibers and then meticulously weaving them on a loom. The geometric patterns and stylized animal figures were often imbued with symbolic meaning, reflecting clan affiliations and spiritual beliefs.

The artistic repertoire also included intricate carvings in other materials, such as bone, shell, and stone. Small, finely detailed carvings of animals, human figures, and supernatural beings were created for use as personal adornments, tools, and ceremonial objects. The aesthetic principles of the Pacific Northwest art are characterized by a strong sense of form, balance, and the use of bold, sweeping lines. The characteristic "formline" design, a double-curved line that forms the basis of many compositions, is a hallmark of the region's artistic style. This formline is often filled with ovoid shapes, U-forms, and S-forms, creating a dynamic and visually engaging aesthetic. The use of vibrant colors, often contrasting reds, blues, greens, and blacks, further enhanced the impact of these artworks.

The spiritual beliefs of the Pacific Northwest peoples were as diverse as the peoples themselves, but common themes often revolved around the interconnectedness of the natural world and the spirit realm. Animals were frequently seen as having supernatural powers and were often revered as ancestors or spirit helpers. The concept of transformation was also prevalent, with myths and stories frequently depicting beings changing from one form to another, such as humans into animals and vice versa. This belief in the fluid boundaries between different states of being was often reflected in the art, where figures might be depicted in a transitional state, incorporating elements of multiple creatures. Ceremonies and rituals played a crucial role in maintaining the balance between the human and spirit worlds, and these often involved elaborate costumes, masks, and performances that brought mythological beings to life. The masks, in particular, were extraordinary works of art, often made from wood and adorned with feathers, fur, and other materials. They were used in dances and ceremonies to embody ancestral spirits, supernatural beings, and animals, allowing the wearer to channel their power and connect with the spiritual realm. The artistry involved in creating these masks was exceptional, with carvers skillfully capturing the essence of the beings they represented. The dynamic expressions, the intricate details, and the vibrant colors all contributed to their powerful spiritual impact.

The peoples of the Pacific Northwest, through their intimate knowledge of the sea and forests, and their sophisticated social and artistic traditions, created a culture that was both remarkably resilient and vibrantly expressive. Their ingenuity in harnessing the abundant resources of their environment, from the salmon-rich waters to the majestic cedar forests, allowed them to develop complex societies with rich spiritual lives and a deep appreciation for the beauty and power of the natural world. The legacy of their craftsmanship, their social innovations like the potlatch, and their profound connection to the land and sea continues to resonate, offering a powerful testament to human adaptation and cultural richness.

10 | The Great Plains: Nomads of the Grasslands

The Great Plains, a seemingly endless expanse of rolling grasslands stretching across the heart of North America, nurtured a unique and profoundly adaptable set of cultures. This vast territory, characterized by its sweeping vistas and fertile soil, became the ancestral home to numerous Indigenous peoples, including the ancestors of the Lakota, Cheyenne, Pawnee, and many others. Life on the plains was a testament to ingenuity, a constant dance between human resourcefulness and the powerful rhythms of nature. At the very center of this existence, both physically and spiritually, was the majestic bison, often referred to as buffalo. This magnificent creature was far more than just a food source; it was the lifeblood of the plains peoples, providing sustenance, shelter, and the very materials that shaped their material world.

Before the arrival of Europeans and the transformative introduction of the horse, the inhabitants of the Great Plains had already developed sophisticated strategies for survival in this challenging yet bountiful environment. Their movements were dictated by the seasons and the migratory patterns of the bison herds, creating a nomadic lifestyle that was both practical and deeply connected to the land. These groups were not aimlessly wandering; their journeys were purposeful, following ancient trails that led to prime grazing lands and abundant hunting grounds. While the bison roamed, so too did the people, their lives a fluid ebb and flow across the grasslands. This nomadic existence fostered a remarkable sense of community and interdependence, as families and bands relied on each other for survival, especially during hunts and the harsh winter months. Their knowledge of the plains was encyclopedic, encompassing an intimate understanding of plant life, water sources, weather patterns, and, most importantly, the behavior of the bison. This deep ecological knowledge was crucial for their sustained presence and success on the plains.

The bison provided an almost inexhaustible larder. Its meat, when dried and pounded into pemmican, could be stored for long periods, providing essential protein and fat for sustenance throughout the year. This preservation technique was vital for surviving lean times and for supporting long journeys. The thick hide of the bison was a treasure trove of material. It was tanned and transformed into durable clothing, including leggings, shirts, and moccasins, offering protection from the elements. More significantly, the hides were used to create the iconic **tipis** (sometimes spelled tepees), the portable dwellings that defined the Plains cultures. These conical structures, made from numerous bison hides stretched over a framework of wooden poles, were ingeniously designed for nomadic life. They were remarkably stable in high winds, easy to erect and dismantle, and provided excellent insulation, keeping inhabitants warm in winter and relatively cool in summer. The central opening at the top of the tipi could be adjusted to control ventilation and allow smoke from the cooking fire to escape, while also providing a view of

the sky, which held deep spiritual significance for many plains peoples. The construction and maintenance of tipis were communal efforts, further strengthening social bonds. A single tipi could house an entire family, and entire villages of tipis would be erected in sheltered locations, often near water sources and good grazing land for the bison. The arrangement of tipis within a village also held social meaning, reflecting kinship ties and community structure.

Hunting the bison was a communal undertaking, requiring immense skill, courage, and cooperation. In the pre-horse era, these hunts were often conducted on foot, a testament to the incredible agility and strategic thinking of the plains hunters. They developed a variety of techniques to bring down these powerful animals. One common method involved driving herds into natural corrals, such as canyons or arroyos, where they could be more easily dispatched. Another strategy was the use of disguised hunters who would approach the herds, often adorned with bison hides, mimicking the animals to get close enough for a kill with spears or atlatls (a spear-throwing device that increased leverage and distance). Sometimes, hunters would stampede herds over cliffs, a dangerous but effective method for killing large numbers of bison at once. The success of a hunt was not just about individual skill; it was a collective achievement that ensured the survival and prosperity of the entire community. Every part of the bison was utilized, reflecting a profound respect for the animal and a commitment to avoiding waste. Beyond meat and hides, bones were fashioned into tools and implements, such as awls, scrapers, and projectile points. Sinew was used for lashing and sewing, and even the stomach lining could be used as a container. This holistic utilization of the bison embodied a deep ecological wisdom and a sustainable way of life.

The advent of the horse, introduced by Europeans and gradually adopted by Plains peoples through trade and capture, revolutionized life on the Great Plains. While the pre-horse era demonstrates incredible adaptation, the horse brought about an even greater degree of mobility and efficiency. The horse allowed for larger hunting parties, swifter pursuits, and the ability to cover vast distances with greater ease. This increased mobility contributed to the intensification of nomadic lifestyles and, in some instances, led to the consolidation of certain groups into larger bands or tribes. Hunting strategies evolved, with mounted hunters now able to pursue bison at a gallop, using bows and arrows with deadly accuracy. The horse became an integral part of Plains culture, not just as a mode of transportation but as a symbol of wealth, status, and prestige. Owning many horses was a sign of prosperity, and raiding for horses became an important aspect of intertribal relations, often serving as a means of asserting dominance or acquiring wealth. However, it is crucial to remember that for many millennia, these cultures thrived without the horse, demonstrating their inherent resilience and resourcefulness. Their sophisticated hunting techniques and nomadic patterns were well-established long before their arrival.

Beyond the material aspects of life, the cultures of the Great Plains were rich in spiritual and social traditions. Oral traditions played a paramount role in transmitting knowledge, history, and cultural values from one generation to the next. Storytelling was a revered art form, with elders recounting tales of creation, heroic deeds, ancestral journeys, and the wisdom of the natural world. These stories often served as both entertainment and education, instilling a deep understanding of their heritage and their place within the cosmos. Ceremonies were central to Plains life, marking significant events such as births, coming-of-age rituals, successful hunts, and seasonal changes. The Sun Dance, perhaps one of the most sacred and widely practiced ceremonies, was a profound expression of spiritual devotion, sacrifice, and a plea for the well-being of the community and the abundance of the bison herds. This elaborate ceremony, often involving fasting, prayer, and sometimes self-mortification, was a powerful affirmation of their connection to the spiritual realm and the life-giving forces of the universe. Other ceremonies involved vision quests, where individuals would seek spiritual guidance and strength through solitude and prayer, often in remote locations.

Social organization on the Plains varied among different groups, but commonalities existed. Kinship ties were fundamental, with families and extended kin forming the basic social units. Bands, composed of related families, would often travel and hunt together. Leadership within these bands was typically based on merit, wisdom, generosity, and prowess in hunting and warfare. Chiefs were respected for their ability to guide and protect their people, but their authority was often consensual rather than absolute. Decisions were frequently made through councils, where men and sometimes women would voice their opinions and contribute to collective decision-making. The concept of reciprocity was deeply ingrained in their social fabric, extending beyond the immediate family to encompass the entire community. Sharing resources, especially during times of need, was not just an act of charity but a fundamental principle of social cohesion. This emphasis on cooperation and mutual support was essential for survival in the challenging environment of the Great Plains, fostering a strong sense of collective identity and shared destiny. The intricate balance between individual freedom and communal responsibility, a hallmark of Plains cultures, allowed them to adapt and thrive for centuries.

The material culture, though seemingly simple due to its nomadic nature, was remarkably sophisticated and beautifully crafted. Beyond the tipi and bison hide garments, artisans created intricate beadwork, quillwork, and painted designs that adorned clothing, shields, and other personal belongings. These decorative elements were not merely ornamental; they often carried symbolic meaning, representing clan affiliations, spiritual beliefs, or personal achievements. Geometric patterns, stylized representations of animals, and abstract designs were common motifs, executed with a keen eye for color and composition. The tools and weapons, while functional, were also crafted with care and artistry. The deep spiritual connection to the natural world permeated every aspect of their lives, from the way they hunted and gathered to the stories they told and the art they created. The Great Plains, with its vast grasslands and abundant bison, provided the canvas upon which these remarkable cultures painted a legacy of resilience, adaptability, and profound connection to the earth.

11 | The Inuit: Surviving the Arctic North

The vast, frozen expanse of the Arctic North, a realm of perpetual ice, biting winds, and long, dark winters, might seem to us an inhospitable and desolate place. Yet, for the Inuit people, this extreme environment was, and remains, their ancestral homeland. Their story is one of unparalleled resilience, ingenuity, and a profound, almost symbiotic relationship with one of the planet's most challenging landscapes. For millennia, the Inuit have not merely survived in the Arctic; they have thrived, developing a rich culture and a sophisticated way of life perfectly attuned to the rhythms of the ice, the sea, and the sparse, hardy life that exists there. This remarkable adaptation is a testament to human perseverance and the extraordinary capacity for innovation when faced with the absolute necessity of survival.

The Inuit, a term meaning "the people" in their own language, encompass a wide range of related groups spread across the Arctic regions of North America, including Greenland, Canada, and Alaska. Their territories are characterized by tundra, glaciers, and vast stretches of sea ice, a world dominated by white and blue, where the sun dips below the horizon for months on end. It is a landscape that demands respect, deep knowledge, and a constant vigilance against the ever-present dangers of cold, starvation, and the unforgiving nature of the elements. Unlike the nomadic peoples of the Great Plains, whose movements were dictated by the migrations of bison across open grasslands, the Inuit's existence was inextricably linked to the sea and the seasonal changes of the ice. Their strategies for survival were honed over thousands of years, passed down through generations, becoming the very fabric of their culture.

At the heart of Inuit survival was their mastery of hunting. The Arctic is not a land of abundant plant life that can sustain large populations year-round, but it teems with marine mammals and land animals that provided the essential resources for life. Seals, in particular, were a cornerstone of the Inuit diet and lifestyle. These sleek, blubber-rich creatures offered not only vital nourishment but also fat for lamps that provided light and warmth, hides for clothing and shelter, and bones for tools. Hunting seals required immense patience, skill, and an intimate understanding of their behavior. Inuit hunters would often wait for hours, sometimes days, at seal breathing holes in the ice, motionless and silent, their harpoons poised. They learned to read the subtle signs of a seal's presence – the disturbance of snow, the faint scent, the slight shift in the ice. The successful harpoon strike, followed by a fierce struggle to haul the heavy catch onto the ice, was a triumph that could sustain a family for days. They also developed specialized techniques for hunting seals in their kayaks, sleek, agile boats designed for maneuvering in icy waters.

Beyond seals, the Inuit also hunted whales, a more challenging but incredibly rewarding endeavor. These hunts were often communal affairs, requiring coordinated efforts and the use of larger boats called umiaks, which could carry multiple hunters and their gear. Whale blubber was a highly prized source of fat and calories, and the meat provided sustenance. The bones and sinew were also utilized for tools and construction. On land, the caribou provided another crucial resource. These migratory animals offered meat, hides, and bones, similar to the bison on the plains, but adapted to the Arctic environment. The Inuit developed sophisticated methods for hunting caribou, including driving them into natural traps or ambushes, and utilizing their knowledge of caribou migration routes to intercept them. Even smaller game, like arctic hares and birds, and the fish from rivers and lakes contributed to the diverse diet, demonstrating the Inuit's ability to extract sustenance from every available niche.

The extraordinary cold of the Arctic demanded equally extraordinary adaptations in clothing. The Inuit developed a system of dressing in layers of animal skins that was remarkably effective at trapping body heat and protecting against the elements. The most iconic of these garments are the parkas, often made from caribou or seal skins, with hoods designed to be pulled up tightly around the face, sometimes with a ruff of fur to further shield the wearer from wind and snow. The unique design of the Inuit parka, with its loose-fitting outer layer and snugger inner layer, allowed for excellent insulation and freedom of movement. The waterproofing of seal skins was

particularly valuable for outer garments worn during hunting or travel in wet conditions. The fur of the caribou, with its hollow hairs, provided exceptional warmth, making it ideal for the inner layers. Moccasins, mittens, and trousers were all crafted with the same meticulous attention to detail, utilizing every part of the animal hide to create durable, warm, and functional clothing. The skill of Inuit women in preparing these hides and stitching these garments was paramount to the survival of their communities, a testament to their vital role in Arctic life.

Shelter was another critical aspect of Inuit adaptation. While often associated with the snow house, or igloo, this was not their only form of dwelling, nor was it always a permanent structure. Igloos were ingeniously constructed from blocks of snow, carefully cut and fitted together to create a dome that was surprisingly strong and an excellent insulator. The shape of the igloo allowed for the efficient trapping of body heat and the warmth from a small oil lamp, creating a relatively comfortable living space even in the harshest blizzards. The entrance was often designed with a tunnel, which helped to keep the warmer air inside and the colder air out. However, igloos were more commonly used as temporary shelters during hunting expeditions or when traveling across the ice. For more permanent settlements, especially during the summer months, the Inuit would erect tents made from caribou hides stretched over wooden or whalebone frames. These structures were also designed for efficiency and portability, allowing the people to move with the seasons and the availability of resources.

The Inuit's mastery of transportation was equally vital for their survival and their ability to exploit the vast Arctic landscape. The kayak, a single-person, enclosed boat, was a marvel of design. Made from a wooden frame covered with seal skins, it was lightweight, agile, and incredibly stable in rough seas. Inuit hunters used kayaks to pursue seals and other marine animals with remarkable efficiency, their ability to paddle silently and maneuver with precision being key to their success. For transporting larger groups of people, hunting equipment, or supplies, the umiak, a larger, open boat also constructed from animal skins stretched over a frame, was indispensable. On land, the Inuit developed the dog sled, a sturdy and efficient mode of transport across the snow and ice. Teams of trained sled dogs, bred for strength and endurance, could pull heavy loads over long distances, allowing the Inuit to travel between hunting grounds, visit other communities, and transport their families and belongings. The development of the wide, flat runners on the sleds helped to distribute the weight and prevent them from sinking too deeply into the snow.

The spiritual beliefs of the Inuit were deeply interwoven with the harsh realities of their environment. Their cosmology recognized the interconnectedness of all things, from the animals they hunted to the spirits of the land, sea, and sky. The shaman, or angakkuq, played a crucial role in Inuit society, acting as a mediator between the human and spirit worlds. Through rituals and trance states, shamans would seek to understand and influence the forces that governed their lives, such as the weather, the success of hunts, and the health of the community. They would appease spirits, heal the sick, and guide those who had strayed from the proper path. Beliefs about the sea goddess Sedna, who controlled the animals of the ocean and could cause famine if displeased, were central to many Inuit communities. Offerings and respectful hunting practices were seen as essential to maintain harmony with the natural world and ensure a continued supply of food. Dreams and visions were also considered important channels of spiritual communication, providing guidance and insight.

The concept of reciprocity and respect for the animal world was fundamental to Inuit culture. They believed that animals possessed spirits and that it was essential to treat them with respect, to use every part of a hunted animal, and to avoid waste. This reverence for the animals that sustained them was not just a spiritual practice; it was a practical necessity for ensuring the long-term viability of their resources. Rituals and taboos surrounding hunting and butchering were designed to honor the animals and maintain a balance with the natural world. This deep ecological understanding, developed over millennia of observation and interaction, allowed the Inuit to live sustainably in an environment where resources were often scarce and unpredictable.

The social structure of Inuit communities, while varying across different regions, was generally characterized by a strong emphasis on cooperation and mutual support. Extended families formed the core social unit, with individuals relying on each other for survival, especially during the challenging winter months. Sharing of resources, particularly food, was a fundamental principle. A successful hunter was expected to share their catch with the entire community, ensuring that no one went hungry. This communal spirit was essential for navigating the unpredictable nature of Arctic life, where a single hunting failure could have devastating consequences for a family. Leadership was often informal, based on experience, skill, and the ability to provide for the group, rather than on inherited status or formal authority. Elders were highly respected for their wisdom and knowledge, and their advice was often sought.

The ingenuity of the Inuit extended to their tools and technology. The harpoon, with its detachable head, was a crucial innovation for hunting marine mammals. Knives and scrapers made from bone, ivory, and stone were essential for preparing hides, butchering animals, and crafting other tools. The development of oil lamps, carved from soapstone and fueled by animal fat, provided a vital source of light and heat, making life in the long winter nights bearable. The use of bone and ivory for crafting intricate tools, weapons, and decorative objects demonstrated a remarkable artistic sensibility and a deep understanding of the materials available to them. Their ability to create durable and functional items from such limited resources is a testament to their resourcefulness.

The arrival of Europeans and other outsiders brought profound changes to Inuit life, introducing new technologies, diseases, and economic systems that disrupted their traditional ways of life. However, the enduring spirit of the Inuit, their deep connection to their homeland, and their incredible capacity for adaptation continue to define their culture. The story of the Inuit is a powerful reminder of the strength and resilience of the human spirit in the face of extreme environmental challenges, and a compelling testament to the diverse and innovative ways in which people have learned to live in harmony with the Earth. Their ability to thrive in one of the planet's most formidable environments speaks volumes about their wisdom, their resourcefulness, and their profound understanding of the natural world.

12 | The Great Law of Peace: Iroquois Confederation

The wind howls across the plains, carrying stories of ancient times, of conflicts that raged and then, miraculously, subsided. In the heart of what is now New York State, and extending into parts of Canada, a remarkable transformation occurred among a group of Indigenous nations known collectively as the Haudenosaunee, or the Iroquois. For generations, these peoples—the Mohawk, Oneida, Onondaga, Cayuga, and Seneca—had lived in a state of perpetual tension, their lands often marked by the shadows of intertribal warfare. However, a profound vision of peace and unity emerged, leading to the formation of one of the most sophisticated political structures in the pre-Columbian Americas: the Iroquois Confederacy, guided by what is known as the Great Law of Peace.

The establishment of the Confederacy, often referred to as the "Great Binding Law," is traditionally placed around the mid-15th century, though archaeological evidence suggests its roots may extend even earlier. It was not a sudden event, but a gradual process driven by a powerful need to end the relentless cycle of violence that had plagued the region. The constant conflict not only caused immense suffering but also weakened the nations, making them vulnerable to external threats and hindering their collective progress. Imagine the constant anxiety, the need for vigilance, the loss of loved ones, and the disruption to daily life that such warfare entailed. It was a heavy burden that the Haudenosaunee carried for too long.

The catalyst for this monumental change is often attributed to the wisdom and diplomacy of a spiritual leader named Skennenrahawi, often translated as "The Peacemaker." According to oral traditions, Skennenrahawi traveled from nation to nation, carrying a message of peace and a vision for a unified people. He spoke of a time when the nations would lay down their weapons, bury the hatchet, and instead of warring against each other, would work together for the common good. His teachings emphasized the interconnectedness of all beings, the importance of mutual respect, and the strength that comes from unity. He envisioned a council fire where representatives from all the nations could gather, deliberate, and make decisions together, ensuring that the voices of all were heard.

The process of forming the Confederacy was not without its challenges. Each nation had its own traditions, its own leaders, and its own history of grievances. Skennenrahawi's task was to persuade them to set aside their differences and embrace a new way of life. He used powerful metaphors and compelling arguments, painting a vivid picture of a future where their combined strength would ensure their prosperity and security. He spoke of the longhouse, a traditional dwelling that housed many families, as a symbol of their union. Within this symbolic longhouse, each nation would have its place, its fire, and its responsibilities, but all would be bound together by the rafters of peace and shared governance.

THE GRAND COUNCIL

The Great Law of Peace, enshrined in the oral traditions and conveyed through intricate wampum belts, laid out the principles and structure of the Confederacy. It established a council of chiefs, known as the Grand Council, composed of representatives from each of the allied nations. These chiefs were not hereditary rulers in the European sense, but were chosen based on their wisdom, integrity, and commitment to the principles of peace. The positions were often held by men, but the selection process involved the clan mothers, the matriarchal leaders who held significant influence within their clans and the nation. This ensured that the voices of the women, who played a crucial role in maintaining the social fabric and well-being of the community, were respected and considered.

A cornerstone of the Great Law of Peace was the principle of consensus-based decision-making. Unlike systems where a simple majority vote could decide an issue, the Grand Council strove for unanimity. Debates were lengthy and thorough, with chiefs carefully considering all perspectives before reaching a decision. If even one chief strongly objected, the matter would be further discussed until a resolution acceptable to all could be found. This commitment to consensus ensured that all nations felt heard and valued, fostering a deep sense of ownership over the decisions made and a strong commitment to upholding them. It was a complex and time-consuming process, but it resulted in decisions that were more robust and widely supported.

The Great Law of Peace also established a framework for justice and conflict resolution. Instead of retaliation, emphasis was placed on restoring balance and harmony. When disputes arose, they were brought before the Grand Council, where elders and chiefs would mediate and seek a resolution that addressed the needs of all parties involved. This focus on restorative justice was a radical departure from the often-retributive systems of justice prevalent elsewhere and was a key factor in the Confederacy's long-term stability. It acknowledged that true peace was not merely the absence of conflict, but the presence of justice and mutual understanding.

The Haudenosaunee Confederacy, at its height, comprised five nations: the Mohawk, the Oneida, the Onondaga, the Cayuga, and the Seneca. Later, the Tuscarora nation joined, making it the Six Nations. Each nation retained a significant degree of autonomy over its internal affairs, but they were bound together by the shared principles and responsibilities outlined in the Great Law of Peace. The Onondaga were often designated as the "Keepers of the Central Fire," tasked with hosting the Grand Council meetings and preserving the Confederacy's records, often through the intricate art of wampum. Wampum belts, made from strings of shell beads, were not just decorative items but served as mnemonic devices, recording treaties, laws, and historical events. The patterns and colors of the beads held specific meanings, allowing the oral traditions to be recalled and transmitted with accuracy across generations.

The formation of the Confederacy had profound implications. It created a powerful political and military alliance that significantly altered the balance of power in the Northeast. The unified Haudenosaunee were able to defend their territories more effectively, engage in more successful trade, and exert considerable influence over neighboring tribes and, later, European colonial powers. Their ability to negotiate as a single entity, speaking with one voice, made them formidable diplomats and resilient survivors. The strength of their confederacy allowed them to not only withstand external pressures but also to expand their influence, becoming a dominant force in the region for centuries.

The ideals embedded within the Great Law of Peace—unity, peace, consensus, and mutual respect—were revolutionary. They provided a model for governance that prioritized collective well-being and long-term stability over the immediate gains of conflict. The Confederacy was a testament to the Haudenosaunee people's capacity for foresight, diplomacy, and profound wisdom. It demonstrated that even in the face of deep-seated animosities, it was possible to forge a lasting peace through dialogue, understanding, and a shared commitment to a higher purpose. This legacy continues to resonate, offering valuable lessons about the principles of good governance, the power of unity, and the enduring pursuit of peace. The story of the Great Law of Peace is a powerful reminder that complex societies can be built not on the foundations of conquest, but on the bedrock of cooperation and shared humanity.

For More Books in This Series, Visit Us at:

https://cronoscreek.com

www.ingramcontent.com/pod-product-compliance
Lightning Source LLC
LaVergne TN
LVHW020048110826
845155LV00029B/681

* 9 7 8 1 9 4 5 5 5 3 0 6 6 *